RESTORING THE FAMILY

Analysis and Comments on the Book

The Spirit of the Family in the Home, City and State

Msgr. Henri Delassus

by

Marian T. Horvat, Ph.D.

ISBN: 0-9726516-0-8
Library of Congress Number: 2003094115
Printed and bound in the United States

Cover: The top three panels of the monumental eight-paneled Jesse Tree window in Notre Dame Cathedral, Chartres. The stained glass window represents the genealogy of the family of Our Lord Jesus Christ.

Tradition in Action, Inc.

P.O. Box 23135

Los Angeles, CA 90023

www.TraditionInAction.org

TABLE OF CONTENTS

HAPPY THE MAN WHO LIVES HIS LIFE IN A TIME WHEN TRADITION REIGNS...

"The life of the individual is one, but if we analyze it, we discover three elements in it, the different forces of three distinct epochs.

"This man already, in a certain sense, lived other existences. He has the sense of already having lived in his grandfathers and great-grandfathers. He finds in himself what they thought. The life of his forebears precedes his own and constitutes the *first* epoch.

"In the *second*, which is the present, the individual's life is, so to speak, the flourishing of the first: I continue the work of my grandfather, and I add my thinking and knowledge to his. I do that which he desired to do and I thus prolong his action on this earth. Ah! How long I have lived on earth – for I already lived many years of infancy in my grandparents, of adolescence in my father, of maturity in my own existence!

"The *third* epoch of life is the one that he loves and gazes at without ceasing: He will live in his son, his nephew, his grandchild. His great-grandfather glimpsed him from afar, through the mists, as he worked, economized and guarded the traditions. In his turn, he looks in the same direction, ahead of him: he thinks, desires and constructs for his grandchild, for those beyond him, even further along the line of the horizon.

"Thus the man who lives in a time when the spirit of tradition reigns is one link in a chain that links many generations. He lives in each of them. He feels that his own life was already prepared for him in the lives of those who preceded him, and that it will continue to live still much longer in those who come after him."

Msgr. J. B. C. Isoard,
Oeuvres Pastorales, Paris, 1884.

FOREWORD

It is my opinion that the American traditionalist and conservative Catholic movements are probably the most important in today's world. Often, one of their characteristics is courage. I will focus on just one point. Because parents objected to the revolutionary path of public schools and the progressivist hues of religious institutions of learning, they refused to send their children to them. From this general reaction the initiative of home-schooling was born. These parents did not fear the fashionable accusations: "Your children will not have companions to socialize with;" or "Your children will not have a diploma after finishing their studies." They cared first about the spiritual and intellectual health of their children; the rest would come. And it did come. The State has already started recognizing these studies pursued at home so that home-schooled students can enroll in universities. Also, and even better, various conservative and traditionalist colleges have been founded here and there to provide a higher education to these youth after high-school. Therefore, the American home-schooling initiative won citizenship. At the beginning of this battle were two principal elements: the Catholic Faith and courage.

The successful American experiment provides a good example to be followed by those European and Latin American Catholics who are also conservatives or traditionalists, but still fearful of social pressures. My intention, however, is not to enter into the moral counsels. I want to point out another interesting consequence of the mentioned initiative.

By taking their children out of those schools and keeping them at home, the parents, perhaps without realizing it entirely, were creating conditions for a Catholic restoration of the family life. Several factors contributed to this fact.

First, this reaction on the whole represented a leap back in Catholic religious formation to a state of things before Vatican II, which means a return of 50 years. As for the general education, this reaction signified a return to a state of things before public schooling became compulsory under law, that is, about 100 years ago. What this return signifies, then, is that children are being raised in a healthy moral milieu, out of the stream of the most recent revolutionary customs and ideas.

Second, when the children are at home, the parents must educate them, the mother during the day, the father after work. This education is no longer the cold and anonymous education of remunerated employees of a distant institution, but a personalized instruction given in an ambience of love and respect. Instead of money to form their children, the parents have to give of themselves, their time and efforts. They have to reserve time to review their old school-books and recall those forgotten rules of grammar so necessary to speak well, those main facts of History indispensable for a clear understanding of the political and social reality, or even those boring laws and formulas of Physics and Chemistry that, however, will allow their children to analyze what is happening in Science today. When a brother or a sister is more advanced, he or she also helps to teach the younger children. Besides the learning at home, which I believe can be more efficient than elsewhere, this familiar instruction is an inestimable factor of psychological stability and security for children who grow up in a warm ambience of consideration.

Third, the confidence of children in their parents increases. Instead of being viewed as merely the ones who pay for their outside education, the parents are seen as teachers, the ones who know and explain for them what are life, religion, history, and science. It is not necessary to stress that this continuity of the same familiar thinking is a powerful factor to avoid conflicts and improve harmony inside a home.

Without the pretension of presenting a complete picture, I simply wanted to exemplify how the Catholic family found a great factor of restoration in the home-schooling movement.

As a traditionalist intellectual leader and educator Dr. Marian T. Horvat has received frequent and numerous requests to offer her contribution to the restoration of the family. Some are questions from parents on how to improve their home-schools; others relate to the moral and social formation of the children; yet others touch on the broader questions about how the Catholic family and society should be constituted. Among the many responsibilities of *Tradition in Action,* of which she is the competent president, she found time to kindly respond to those needs.

The book that is being published now intends to be the first of a series that will give her input on the restoration of a true Catholic family. Other publications will follow, God willing, that will help the members of the family in this noble work. This book is not turned exclusively toward parents and children, teachers and students. Everyone can benefit from it.

Dr. Horvat chose to initiate her series with a basic description of what the Catholic family is. Some of the main reasons for its restoration, as well as several practical suggestions taken from well-known masters on the topic can also be found in her work.

Explaining the principles, she touches on the importance of family traditions for a Catholic home; the significance of maintaining the same house and land to avoid instability and the disappearance of the family; the importance of the authority of the father and the goodness of the mother. But this easy-to-read book does not describe only principles. Along with them are examples and suggestions presented intelligently and pleasantly. How to maintain the history of a family? The *family book* is a suggestion utilized widely in the past. How to avoid family insecurity through the years and generations? The customs of primogeniture and entail are described colorfully. The patriarchal mission of the father and the religious vocation of the mother are also depicted in an admirable way in a chapter by Msgr. Henri Delassus that Dr. Horvat selected to reproduce.

Opportune in its timeliness, fundamental in its importance, counter-revolutionary in its tone, extremely pleasant in its reading, this book is turned toward a wide dissemination.

It is my sincere wish that Our Lady the Queen, on whose feast this work is coming to light, gives it a great influence in the restoration of her Reign.

May 31, 2003
Atila Sinke Guimarães

Chapter I

THE RECONSTITUTION OF THE FAMILY AND THE NEED FOR TRADITION

The lecture on Egyptian civilization had hardly begun when the class was interrupted by a young man, Tim O'Riley by name, who had something he wanted to "share" with the class. This, in itself, explains much about the spirit of many students in the classrooms of the 21st century. Trained to be spontaneous in action, they speak before they think. Influenced by the egalitarian spirit of our age, they imagine their contributions as weighty as the notes prepared by a professor. Lacking judgment that comes from reflection and discipline, they relate personal experiences and feelings with the air of revealing great truths. What Tim O'Riley was impelled to tell the class was that he had made a "personal journey" down the Nile River the summer past and seen the places being described.

"Why did you make this journey?" the professor asked.

Without a blink of the eye, he replied, "It was spiritual, like what you were talking about. I was looking for, like, you know, some traditions. I'm really into the Eastern culture. It's cool."

The irony of our age. A red-haired American of obvious Irish descent makes a personal journey down the Nile to find his traditions as if he were shopping in a mall for a new T-shirt. I wondered if he had ever even thought to look to his own family history for traditions, or to the religion and spirit of Western Civilization to discover his authentic glorious past.

Apparently not. In consequent classes Tim divulged other unsolicited personal revelations: his mother was divorced twice and off in New England somewhere, his father was in an irregular situation with a woman much younger than himself, both of his parents had been Catholic but no longer "practiced." So Tim, age 18, without rudder or anchor, had taken a boat ride down the Nile to "find himself" and some traditions.

The Crisis of the Family and Need for Traditions

What statistics show is that there are increasing numbers of young people in situations like Tim, and many even worse. Everywhere, today we hear about the crisis in the family. One in three marriages end in divorce; the number of "partners" living together without marriage vows is increasing; single-parent households and homosexual and lesbian marriages seem to be on their way to being accepted as a matter of course. The ensuing chaos in society is a natural consequence of this deterioration of the family, the basic organic cell of the social body.

What are the causes for this deterioration of the family? Certainly some of the blame lies on the modern State that sought to replace the authority of the father with that of the State, and to ensure the so-called rights of the individual instead of considering the family and preserving its stability and cohesion.

Obviously, there is a great need for a reconstitution of sound laws based on Catholic moral teaching. But making such laws, which in general lie outside the reach of the average man, constitutes only one part of the task to reconstitute the family.

The other task, which does lie within the reach of each one, is to make the family reborn in traditions.

A guarantee of a people's greatness and stability is their respect for traditions, noted Pius XII in a 1957 speech. This respect, he said, means keeping alive what the centuries have proven to be good and fruitful.[1] Tradition is more than keeping religious feast days and the healthy customs that give unity to a people. It is to follow the moral values and guiding principles that the Catholic Faith instilled in the conscience of a people throughout its history. To respect tradition means to guarantee the moral life of a people.

Without tradition, we have youth like Tim O'Riley, who no longer have clear ideas or principles solidly anchored in souls, but only vague and fluctuating impressions that permit them to float in any direction the wind might take them. Each one is told that he has the right to choose his own principles, make his own destiny, with no need to correspond to a certain way of being or norms of actions. This false liberty that makes Tim O'Riley think that he is sole lord of his present and future, free to change his traditions like he changes the pack he carries on his back, in reality is not liberty. It is an encumbrance that is the fruit of a long process called the Revolution.

His parents also were unconsciously influenced by the same process. This is one reason why they did not create an ambience that would help Tim to grow up organically imbued with his family's traditions, good customs and teaching. Today the guiding principles of how to act and live are no longer impressed on the souls of children

---

[1] Address to professors and students of the *Liceo Ennio Quirino Visonti* of Rome, February 28, 1957.

by parents, who had learned them from the organic teachings of the grandparents, who in turn were imbued by these truths by their ancestors.

We are seeing the sad result of tossing aside the past as "irrelevant" to the present, ignoring the merits of yesterday, revolting against sound moral codes and hierarchy. This state of spirit, instead of giving the happiness and self-fulfillment that was promised, in reality creates a psychological and spiritual emptiness, which produces the great anxiety and instability that characterize men and women – and even children – in society today.

Traditions and the Family Book

In his book on the family, Msgr. Henri Delassus, the famous counter-revolutionary of the late 19th and early 20th centuries, noted while the body of a family is its home and lands that it transmits intact from generation to generation, its soul is constituted by its traditions.[2] Tradition, in the true sense of the word, Delassus continues, is the legacy of the ideas of the ancestors and their sentiments, as well as their organic practices and customs. They find their roots *first*, in the good example and sound morals of the parents, *second*, by the exhortations, counsels and corrections given to the children, and *third,* by *livres de raison*, as the French called them, or, as we would say, the family book.

---

[2] Henri Delassus, *L'esprit familial dans la maison, dans la cité et dans l'Etat* (Lille: Société Saint Augustin, Desclée de Brouwer, 1910, *apud* José Narciso Pinto Soares, *Espírito de família*, Collection Talent de Bien Faire, Barcelos: Companhia Editora do Minho, n.d.). Msgr. Delassus was a relentless polemecist and defender of the Church against the advance of Modernism during the pontificates of Pius IX, Leo XIII, St. Pius X and Benedict XV. One of his better known works is *La conjuration anti-chrétienne*.

The French expression, *livres de raison* [books of reason] is quite appropriate, for this book truly records the reasons and motives for the life of the family. Through it, the family's work, ideas and sentiments are transmitted to the children, and then to the children's children, to guide them on the road of life. It propitiates the transmission of the same family spirit and virtues.

It used to be that each house had its own characteristic that distinguished it. St. Thomas More came from a family of lawyers. Sir Winston Churchill became the stellar star in a constellation of family statesmen. General Douglas MacArthur carried on the military spirit and prowess of his father, Civil War hero Arthur MacArthur. By virtue of distinguishing characteristics, a continuer of the family name felt themselves part of something much greater than each one would be all by himself. He did not have to "find himself" like the unfortunate youth of today. He inherited a certain familiar identity and characteristics, a familiar way of being, that had been formed by his forebears and maintained by tradition.

The family book plays an important role, insists Msgr. Delassus, because it acts as a means of transmission, a tool for this continuity essential to unity. For a father to begin this book, to command his eldest son to continue it and transmit this command to his own son, is the easiest and most secure way to inculcate traditions in a family. It is interesting to note that Msgr. Delassus assumes that it should be the father as the head of the family who should be in charge of the family book, make the entries and moral reflections and practical teachings, and then pass it on to the son who also bear his name.

Today, parents who want to instill traditional - values and establish truly Catholic families often have been so cut off from the past that they hardly have a notion of where to begin. Here, then, is a concrete piece of advice presented by a great counter-revolutionary Monsignor of the last century and offered specifically to the head of the family:

> "May this encourage families that want to go ahead, perpetuate themselves, and re-establish the traditions that made the old aristocracy. Toward this end, let the beautiful custom of family books return in Christian families everywhere. In days past, such books had great prestige in almost all the countries of Europe and even in the East. An institution born spontaneously in so many and diverse countries can only be inspired by nature itself, or better, by the Author of our nature. It was disastrous to abandon it. It would be extremely favorable to recuperate it." [3]

Today we are undoubtedly living in the dark night of Catholic Civilization. Nonetheless, we have a promise along with an aspiration that comes from the deepest and best part of our souls that tells us that a new civilization will be born from the remains of our glorious Catholic past. Our Lady of Fatima came to assure us of her victory. Our Lady of Good Success, centuries before, had already promised the same triumph. It will come, and we will be living stones of this new and majestic Reign of Mary.

Therefore, we have to begin now, with what we have at hand, with what vague memories we retain, with the great aims that Our Lady inspires in souls, to rebuild this new civilization. For parents to reclaim their natural right to educate their children is an important step, one that demands a great dedication and can begin to restore a correct

---

[3] *Ibid.*, p. 133

order, authority and union in the family. Another could be the adoption of the advice of Msgr. Delassus to establish family books.

It is important to keep in mind what Msgr. Delassus means when he says restoration of family. He is not speaking of the modern notion of a nuclear home – mother, father, children, here today, dissolved or dispersed tomorrow. He is speaking of an idea very widespread in times when a Catholic spirit reigned.

> "An almost religious idea," he explains, "was linked to the expression family traditions, understood in the highest sense: an inheritance of truths and virtues, which formed the personages who thus gave to a family house in proportionate measure its duration and grandeur."[4]

He continues:

> "Today, this expression says nothing to new generations who enter the world. They rise on the scene one day to disappear the next, without having received and without leaving after them a whole conjunction of records and sentiments, of principles and customs that in the past were transmitted from father to son and gave families who were faithful to them the possibility of rising in society. The family who possessed traditions generally owed them to its forebear, in whom the sentiment of good was much stronger than in its neighbors and to whom wisdom and a strong will were given in order to inculcate this good in the offspring." [5]

---

[4] *Ibid.*, pp. 126-7.
[5] *Ibid.*

You can see, what Msgr. Delassus is talking about is a family house, a family that will exist not only in the present but in the future, in the sons and grandsons and great-grandsons. For that, a man must do more than make money to provide for the physical needs of his children, and then send them off to college and into the big world all alone to suddenly choose a profession, find their own religion, and make their own way. He must also give them at the same time an intellectual, moral and religious education, which is also not the work of 18 or 21 years, when a child leaves his legal age of minority. It is a work of a lifetime.

Msgr. Delassus has some very beautiful words to say on this, worth attentive consideration:

> "Animals have the strength and resources to satisfy the bodily needs of their offspring, and this suffices for them. But the child, to be moral, has many other needs as well, and it is for this that God gave the parents, in addition to strength, the *authority to educate the will of the children* and set them along the paths of good, remain on them and progress. God desires that this authority be permanent, because moral progress is a work of a whole lifetime.
>
> "And just as, according to the designs of Providence, progress is developed and unfolds over a long period of time, so also it is necessary that the human family not be extinguished with each generation. The family bond must subsist between those who have already died and those who are living, interlacing among themselves all the descendents in a vigorous family line.

"The good man does not think only of his sons, but of the generations that will follow them and strives to make virtue become family tradition." [6]

Interlacing the Past, Present, and Future

What comprises the family book? In his analyses on the family and society in France before the Revolution, Charles de Ribbe collected and studied a multitude of family books of old France and described his findings[7] to serve as models for parents who want to place in practice the examples of their ancestors. In summary, he found that the family book was divided into three parts, corresponding to the three phases of the existence of the family:

- *the past*, which records the genealogy and history of the origins of the family line;
- *the present*, which registers the present day generation;
- *the future*, which is prepared based on the teachings left by the parents and grandparents to their descendents.

Thus, the family book is a kind of mirror that reflects both frontward and backward everything that materially and morally represents the family.

---

[6] *Ibid.*, pp. 127-8.

[7] *Livre de famille* (Paris: Ed. Maison Alfred Mam et Fils, 1879). See also by the same author: *La famille et la société en France avant la Révolution* (Paris: 1879), 2 vols.; *Une famille au XVI siècle* (Paris: Ed. Société Bibliographique, 1882) *apud* H. Delassus, *ibid.*, p. 128-9.

The Past: Genealogy

The first part of the family book is a record of its members. To realize how disconnected we have become from our pasts, it is only necessary to ask a roomful of young persons how many know the names of their grandparents. A few hands might rise. Add the great-grandparents, and it almost sure the air will be empty.

Today, psychologists and therapists are realizing the benefits of making a family tree and "narrative" as a means for self-knowledge and family therapy. The last decades have seen the burgeoning of workshops on "Discovering your roots," and "Knowing Yourself and Your Family." In clinical terms, they explain that beginning to learn about one's heritage can facilitate self-awareness not merely as an individual, but as a member of a group and provide a bridge to a forgotten cultural base.[8]

It is, after all, natural that this should be so. That the family line is important is evident in Holy Scriptures, which present the genealogy of the Holy Family of Nazareth not just once, but twice, *first* in the descending order of generations (Mt 1: 1-17) and the *second* in inverse order (Lk 3:23-33). Joseph and Mary, like all the Hebrews, were conscious of belonging to a family, the family of David. And that family's greatest glory, which distinguished it above all others in the Hebrew nation, was the knowledge that from its stock would come the Messiah. Each member of the house of David, from greatest to smallest, shared in this honor and distinction.

---

[8] Thomas S. Rue, "Genealogy as a tool for self-knowledge and family therapy," 1998, Internet Site: *http://freepages.genealogy.roots.eb.com/ ~tomrue/systems.htm*

It is not necessary to have an extensive family tree or delve into the numerous genealogical records that exist today in order to begin a family book. Let each one begin with what he has. For the restoration of the Catholic family, the *spirit* of the book is as important as the facts. For example, the name of a family member should have a small note entered along with it, naming a distinctive attribute of the person or his contribution to the family. This begins to sketch a family history, which all families should have. And the guardian of that history is the family book.

In these short notes the family can see how frequently their forebears, often modest in means, endured and went ahead for many centuries in the same region by the strength of good customs and the practice of the same virtues. For example, the family book of the Brac family, shows how, over seven generations (16th to 18th centuries), it rose in prominence from a start in leatherworking to eventual high office in regional and Parisian public life. Over the centuries, the family accumulated land (the patrimony), broadened and passed on its professional knowledge, utilized kinship networks to advance various members who showed promise, practiced personal thrift and prudence in their affairs, and stimulated virtuous conduct. Although, through marriages, various lines of the family were geographically dispersed, their activities in the main continued to focus on the ancestral family lands and local society of its origins.[9] This is an example of how a family progresses in an organic society.

From his extensive research, De Ribbe also affirmed this upward motion of the stable family in society:

---

[9] Olivier Zeller, "On the Origins of a Fermier General: Family Strategies over Seven Generations," *The History of the Family*, vol. 3, n. 3, 1995.

"Based on irrefutable testimonies, we can say that
when families walked on the ways traced by God,
conquering the vices and elevating themselves by
virtue, work and thrift, thanks to a serious Christian
education, they always achieved a great material
wealth, which they possessed in a stable manner." [10]

Finally, recording the family names serves a salutary
purpose that can never be stressed enough to its members.
This should remind the family to pray to God for the souls
of their forebears and to honor their memories.

These are lines from the family book of a State
councilor in 17th-century France:

"That our children might know those from whom
they descended on the part of the father and mother,
that they are stimulated to pray for their souls and
praise the memory of those who, by God's grace,
honored their house and acquired the goods that they
have the fruit of and which will be passed on to the
next generation if, in His goodness, the Creator so
desires to grant this blessing, as I supplicate with all
my heart." [11]

The Present: The Important Family Events

After the genealogy comes the diary, or archives,
where the important acts of the family are registered suc-
cessively:

---

[10] *La Famille et la sociéte en France, apud* H. Delassus, *Ibid.*, p. 133.
[11] *Ibid.*, p. 130

- Births, marriages, and deaths, with any information that belongs to each one of these facts;
- financial records, the material goods of the family, with registered copies of property titles and deeds, the account and business books;
- the family donations and offerings to the Church and her institutions.

Here again, the father aims at more than a mere listing of goods. When possible, he includes an exposition of work methods and counsels based on his own experience that can better the fortune of the family. The example of the parent's fidelity to duty is thus recorded and guarded in the family book, as witness for the children, inviting them to assume the same profession, practice the same industry and provide the same education for their own sons and daughters.

To exhort his own descendents to continue an honorable family name, one man wrote this:

> "You will find, my children, a long sequence of esteemed parents, well considered and honored in their region and by all their neighbors. An honest existence, a medium fortune, but a reputation without stain: behold the capital that they transmitted for 400 years, eleven good parents of families, who never abandoned the name that they received nor the country in which they were born." [12]

Eleven generations of an unstained family name! Eleven generations of Catholic parents practicing virtue and instilling a respect and love for those values in their

---

[12] *Ibid.*, p. 100.

children. This is, indeed, a grand legacy, and one that
would be difficult to find today.

Here is another entry after a listing of accounts that
explains the great importance a family placed on retaining
the goods left to their members and not squandering them
in luxury or self interest:

> "Beloved children, we can sell and disperse our
> goods, but should we do so, we would only consume
> their fruits. Our goods are in our hands with the end
> of working indefatigably to increase them and trans-
> mit them to those who will follow us in the course of
> life. The one who dissipates the patrimony makes a
> despicable robbery, because he betrays the
> confidence of the parents and dishonors the children.
> It would have been better for him and all his lineage
> not to have been born. I warn you, then, against con-
> suming the goods of your children and covering your
> name in infamy." [13]

The good man thinks not only of his sons, but also
of the generations that will follow them. He strives not
only to better the family's condition, but also to make virtue and sound living become a family tradition.

The Future: Ideas and Moral Reflections

Clearly, moral reflections and teachings accom-
pany each part of a well-made Catholic *livre de raison*.
But the third part of the family book places special emphasis on such counsels of the parents. Here they leave the
wisdom gained through the practical experience of their

---

[13] *Ibid.*

lives that they judge worthwhile for their descendents. Here is the opportunity to tell the children: See, I learned from this experience that this good course is the one to follow. Likewise, always avoid this error, be vigilant against this fault that can bring you disgrace and even perdition.

This advice, quite often formulated with or accompanied by words taken from Sacred Scripture, is short. A father should meditate on what he wants to say, with the hope that his words will engrave themselves firmly in his children's minds and penetrate the depths of their hearts.

In the *Instruction* the great St. Louis IX wrote to his son, one sees that his first concern is to pass on the virtue of justice, which he loves above all others and that stands as the *leitmotif* of his personality and reign. He wrote: "My beloved son, if you come to reign, do what is befitting to a king, that is, be so just as to deviate in nothing from justice, whatever may befall you."[14]

He goes on to give precise instructions on how to assure justice for the poor and counsels his son to never keep anything unjustly acquired.

From the book of Antoine de Couston came this summary of its function:

> "I would like to call this book the wisdom of the family. It must be continued to be written by each generation, as the depository of our successes as well as our errors, thus benefiting those who will come, linking the generations to one another, transforming them into one single family, always alive and animated by the same spirit. If it were not like this, the

---

[14] James J. Walsh, *The Thirteenth: The Greatest of Centuries*, (Albany, NY, 1989), p. 294.

generations would unroll one after the other in a cir-
cle of ignorance and error." [15]

In this part of the family book the role of the father
as its head and voice stands out with particular relevance.
When families were strong and sound, it was frequent to
find thoughts like those of Etienne Pasquier:

> "We should consider our fathers as Gods on earth,
> who were given to us not only to transmit life to us
> and conserve it, but also to sanctify us by a wise in-
> struction." [16]

At the end of his research on the family books of
old France, Charles de Ribbe came to a conclusion demonstrated by experience: If sound societies are the image of
the families that compose it, he said, the sound and healthy
families are, in their turn, those in which paternal authority
is exercised. The more time passes, the more we become
aware that it is necessary to return to the family its autonomy, and to the father his authority. [17]

The restoration of the family book that includes the
wise counsels of fathers to sons can be one means to this
end.

---

[15] De Ribbe, *La famille, apud ibid.*, p. 131.

[16] *Oeuvres choisies*, Ed. Firmin-Didto, Paris, 1849, *apud ibid.*, p. 136.

[17] De Ribbe, *La famille, apud ibid.*, p. 137.

Chapter II

THE FAMILY PATRIMONY

At the end of the 19th century the following conversation was overheard between the marquis of an old estate and his workman.

The latter said with no small pride, "In the past month of December, I completed 347 years of service with Your Excellency."

The marquis, after thanking his faithful servant, stated, "But we were here before you. I am not sure of the exact time, but certainly it is more than 600 years."[18]

This short but noteworthy conversation contains many lessons for those who are interested in understanding some of the principles of Catholic organic society.

First, we find the polite forms of address and manner of a non-egalitarian Catholic society. Here exists an unabashed social class system, represented by a noble and a worker. But, lo, to the surprise of ears accustomed to the revolutionary jargon that all inequalities create bitterness and unrest, we see no tortured resentments or hatred of the "oppressed" for the "oppressor," but rather, a mutual respect of master and servant for the station and dignity of each, a pride in the continuity of their respective family situations, and the natural warmth, security and serenity of spirit that such a long relationship of two families normally generates.

---

[18] J.B.C. Iosard, *Oeuvres pastorales* (Paris, 1884), *apud* H. Delassus, *ibid.*, p. 95.

Second, one notes the great stability of place that was a fruit of Christian Civilization, a factor central to the stability of the family and society itself. Today the situation is much different. We are living in times when statistics tell us that one out of five families will move in the next five years. Postal records show approximately 40 million change-of-addresses registered every year. Studies detail the disastrous effects of this unsettling mobility on both children and parents.

Contrast this with our example from the past: for almost 350 years, a family worked in the same place, passing down a trade as well as a home for generation after generation. When the servant said "I completed 347 years of service with Your Excellency," the "I" meant my family. It is remarkable.

The marquis's reply is also admirable: "We have been here for more than 600 years!" By "we," he also meant much more than himself as an individual; he meant his family as a unit that extends from the past and goes into the present, preparing for the future. To maintain the unity and continuity through the centuries, a family was a whole community with, so to speak, a single body and soul. This confirms what we saw in the first chapter, that the soul of the family is tradition: the family customs, religious practices, sentiments, and ideas of the ancestors conserved and passed down through the family book.

And what would be the body of the family? It is the patrimony of the family – the family home and goods – that each generation received from its grandparents as a sacred deposit. He conserved it religiously, strengthened it by adding to it when he could, and then transmitted it faithfully to the next generation. The family is similar to a beehive, noted Msgr. Delassus in his work: the bees are born and die in it; but the beehive remains.[19]

A man, the Church has always taught, has a natural right to property, and when this man is the head of a family this right becomes stronger, because his natural duty and instinct is to create a patrimony for his offspring.[20] To safeguard this right, Christian Civilization elaborated many laws, customs and juridical institutes of admirable wisdom.

---

[19] H. Delassus, *ibid.*, p. 106.

[20] In the Encyclical *Rerum novarum* Pope Leo XIII summarizes with admirable precision the teaching of the Church on the right of property and inheritance: "That right to property, therefore, which has been proved to belong naturally to individual persons, must in likewise belong to a man in his capacity of head of a family; nay, that right is all the stronger in proportion as the human person receives a wider extension in the family group. Nature does not impose on the father of a family only the sacred duty to provide food and all necessaries for those whom he has begotten; it goes further. Just as the children reflect the physiognomy of their father and are a type of continuation of his person, nature inspires him to provide for their future and create a patrimony to help and defend them against all the surprises of bad fortune amid the uncertainties of this mortal life. Now, in no other way can a father effect this except by the ownership of productive property, which he can transmit to his children by inheritance. A family, no less than a civil society, is, as we have said, a true society, governed by an authority peculiar to itself, that is to say, by the authority of the father.

"Provided, therefore, the limits which are prescribed by the very purposes for which it exists be not transgressed, the family enjoys at least equal rights with the State in the choice and pursuit of the things it needs for its preservation and just liberty. We say, 'at least equal rights'; for, inasmuch as the domestic household is antecedent, as well in idea as in fact, to the gathering of men into a community, the family must necessarily have rights and duties which are prior to those of the community, and founded more immediately in nature. If the citizens, on entering into association and fellowship, were to experience hindrance in a commonwealth instead of help, and were to find their rights attacked instead of being upheld, society would rightly be an object to avoid rather than to seek" (n. 13).

Some of these safeguards, such as the customs and laws of entail and primogeniture,[21] may seem archaic, even repulsive to modern minds infected with the egalitarian spirit and complacent toward the socializing tendencies of our age. My point here is not to argue their immediate and unconditional return, but rather to point out their great value in guaranteeing stability and preserving the spirit of family. What is truly necessary is to restore in our hearts the noble sentiments that inspired those customs and institutions of the past and the stable relations in society they produced. When new customs are born following those models, they will be adapted to the circumstances of our times.

The Family Home: A Pillar of Stability

The family has two pillars, said Delassus. One is tradition, and the other is the family patrimony, that is, the family home and the material goods of the family.[22] Both were smashed by the leveling laws that came from the French Revolution, which attacked the patrimony directly, and family tradition as a consequence. The French Civil Code gave a mortal blow to the transmission of the family estate by decreeing the equal division of the patrimony to the children.[23]

---

[21] Under the custom of entail, landed property could not be sold, but only bequeathed (usually to the eldest son). The custom of primogeniture conferred rights to inherit property on the first-born male in the family.

[22] H. Delassus, *ibid.*, p. 98.

[23] The right of primogeniture in inheritance was abolished by the revolutionary legislature. Early acts of the French Legislative Assembly (March 15, 1790) did away this old form of inheritance according to which the head of family transmitted his estates to a single heir, generally his eldest son. The next years, all legal inequalities among the dif-

What did this mean for the traditional family? Msgr. Delassus explains:

"With its stability, spirit of union, traditions of work and austere living, the family estate, where a long sequence of generations of honest persons had been formed, became a truly venerable social institution, truly Catholic. For this reason, it was the object of respect and veneration of all.

"Today the patriarchal home place does not merit this name, because it ceased to be the permanent and stable seat of paternity. As soon as the parents die, it is sold, so its price can be divided. The land is also sold with it; this, as small as it might be, becomes the object of innumerable resentments and quarrels among the surviving family members, who dispute over their small parcels. The fragments are disposed of like barren seed. The children with difficulty manage to escape the consequences of that inevitable destruction. The family is thus condemned to the nomad state and ends fatally by being dissolved." [24]

Primogeniture and entails were juridical customs of Christian civilization that facilitated enormously the survival of the family through the centuries by keeping property in the hand of the same family, generation after generation. The best way to do this proved to be to entail all or a significant part of the land, so that the holder could not sell it, divide it, or even give it away. In the case of primo-

---

ferent heirs were done away with. The *Civil Code* of Napoleon, which inspired many others in Europe and Americas, continued the revolutionary legislature. Kropotkin, *The Great French Revolution, 1789-1793* (NY: Vanguard Printing, 1927), chap. 51.

[24] *Ibid.*, p. 102.

geniture, protected by law should the father leave no will, all the property or the major portion of it would turn over to the eldest son, thus preserving the familiar patrimony.

A common misconception, encouraged by a revolutionary propaganda, is that this system of inheritance was unjust for the younger children, who would always be disfavored and set aside, while the eldest son who inherited reaped the benefits of a life of luxury. It is a false notion on two counts.

First, it is useful to stress that if, on one hand the eldest son had the right to inherit the major part of family's property, on the other, he was responsible for the family's sustenance, education and moral support. Generally speaking, for a half century he would be responsible for the education and good placement of two generations, that of his sisters and brothers and that of their children. In fact, in colonial America this inheritance practice was called the *"favored heir plus burdens,"* indicating the network of obligations to mothers and less favored siblings, that included caring for aged kin, granting use-rights to the estate, and paying legacies out of future revenues.[25]

Second, from the beginning of the spread of primogeniture in the 12th century, there was no one rigid system whereby the eldest son always inherited everything, although this was the general pattern. The first born seemed indicated by Providence to assist the parents, provide for the education of his brothers and sisters, and bear the responsibility of guarding the common interests of the family. Nevertheless, it fell to the authority of the parents to judge who was more capable of carrying on the family work. A son who led a dissipated life could be disinherited

---

[25] Gordon Wood, *Radicalism of the American Revolution* (New York: Vintage Books, 1993), pp. 46-7.

to give a property to a daughter and her husband. An elder son could be set aside for a younger one.[26]

A wide pattern of inheritance also emerged as regions and countries adapted to varying situations. For example, in Bavaria as in certain regions of France, the system of *ultimogeniture* evolved, whereby the father left his property to the youngest son. The reason for this was to ensure the greatest stability for the family by reducing the number of property transfers to the least number possible.

In all cases, what each family ultimately sought was the best means to perpetuate itself, prosper and grow. The goods it handed down intact were those in which the spirit of the family was impressed in the most characteristic way. From generation to generation, the entail was transmitted from father to son, as a living symbol of the qualities and virtues of the family.

In a general way, the other children inherited certain lesser portions or shares of the family goods. As has been confirmed by numerous literature, exclusion of the younger siblings was rarely if ever total, and usually meant only exclusion from the land, with provision in money as a partial compensation. In many cases, joint enfeoffments and family trusts in well-established families amply provided for younger sons.[27]

---

[26] G.S. Becker, A Treatise on the Family (Cambridge: Harvard University Press, 1981); C. Y. C. Chu, "Primogeniture," *Journal of Political Economy,* N. 99, 1991, pp. 78-99; G. Bertocchi, "The law of primogeniture and the transition from landed aristocracy to industrial democracy," January 2003, working paper, Universitá de Modena e Reggio Emilia, pp. 4-5.

[27] G. Bertrocchi, "The Law of Primogeniture," *ibid.*; J. Goody, J. Thirsk and E. P. Thompson, eds., *Family and Inheritance. Rural Society in Western Europe 1200-1800* (Cambridge University Press, 1976); J. P. Labatut, *Les noblesses européennes de la fin du XVe à la fin du XVIIIe Siècle*, (Paris: Presses Universitaires de France, 1978).

At any rate, conserving the family estate intact was a kind of insurance for each family member, who could always count on the support of the family home should he find himself insolvent or in need. To those who preferred not to marry and remain in the paternal home, it offered the serenity of the celibate life lived amid the consolations of a family environment. The family house and patrimonial dominion were the object of a type of perpetual trust, a guarantee of the stability of the family. Both practical matters and the honor of the family name required that it not be permitted to diminish and that all work diligently and live austerely and honorably to make it prosper for the benefit of all.

A custom that developed in Navarre admirably expresses the love that should be had for the principle of conserving the family patrimony. If an owner of a traditional family property died without any apparent heirs, at the moment when his goods were sold to a third party, the bells of the local Church were rung in the funereal fashion, lamenting the death in this case not just of a man, but of a family.[28]

The Individual *versus* the Family in Society

"The state that surged from the French Revolution robbed the family of its independence by means of laws that reduced its right to the advantage of the individual," affirmed Msgr. Delassus. "We are suffering from the deleterious action of the laws and customs, inspired by sophisms of Rousseau, who only had in view the individual,

---

[28] "O direito de herança," *Circular aos propagandistas de Catolicismo*, November, 1956, n. 6.

who only worked for the individual, instead of considering the family and striving to reconstitute it."[29]

By imposing by law the equal partition of property to children, he continued, the *Civil Code* of Napoleon, which inspired many of the emerging modern constitutions of European countries, contributed powerfully to the destruction of the family. By forcing the division of the old family estates, this legislation condemned many great families to dissolve after several generations. Further, it made it difficult for the bourgeois families to maintain themselves stably, and made it almost impossible for worker families to change their condition.[30]

But perhaps the greatest change it effected was how it changed the way of viewing the role of the individual in the family and society. The patrimony came to be considered by the children only as spoils to divide, a means to offer the individual the greatest possible advantages and pleasures. Along with the family lands, the children themselves are dispersed, each one making his own way in the world. No longer interested in remaining close to the parents and working gratuitously for the common good of the family, each one seeks his own personal advantages and good.

It is worthwhile to note that the egalitarian and leveling effect of this legislation was something that other revolutionaries had also understood. Martin Luther and other Protestant leaders advocated the egalitarian principles of partible inheritance.[31] Certainly this is an influence of the theological position of Protestantism, which stressed

---

[29] H. Delassus, *ibid.*, p. 99
[30] *Ibid.*
[31] F. J. Sulloway, "Sibling-order Effects," in *International Encyclopedia of the Social and Behavioral Sciences* (Elsevior Science Ltd., 2001), 14062.

the immediacy of the individual to God, and which relied little on the corporate nature of ecclesiastical society or the principle of hierarchical intermediation.

During the height of the controversies raging over Darwin's theory of evolution, Darwin noted that unequal inheritance practices posed a serious impediment to human evolution, and an impediment for destroying his theory of "natural selection." [32] It was necessary, in his opinion, to remove the individual from those relations where he found natural protection, such as the family, so that he might rely on his own efforts and reason in the seething sea of competition.

In our own country, one of the more radical social effects of the American Revolution was its overthrow of traditional features in land laws. In colonial America the laws of entail and primogeniture, which in some States such as Virginia were even stricter than in England, had contributed to the formation of an organic land-holding aristocracy. But fifteen years after the Declaration of Independence, every State had abolished their laws of entail and primogeniture and provided in some form for equality of inheritance.[33]

The significance of destroying the inheritance law in the American Revolution was witnessed by Alexis de Toqueville in his observations on the emerging American Republic:

> "It was the law of inheritance that was the last step to equality... When framed in a particular manner, this law unites, draws together, and vests property and power in a few hands; it causes an aristocracy, so to speak, to spring out of the ground. If formed

---

[32] *Ibid.*

[33] G. Wood, *Radicalism of the American Revolution*, pp. 182-3.

on opposite principles, its action is still more rapid, it divides, distributes and disperses both property and power."[34]

After his tour of the United States in 1831, De Tocqueville was convinced that he had found an open and egalitarian society that had almost totally done away with family, aristocratic and hereditary values. This view is deeply embedded in the American myth: that we are a people basically equal in condition, that each man relies on his own abilities and opportunities to make himself, that the last traces of rank and hereditary distinction were destroyed in America.

In fact, the reality was, and is, quite different.

Modern scholarship is showing that beneath a veneer of equality and the strong propaganda proclaiming it, American society is hierarchical.[35] And perhaps no other criterion is as important in determining social status as that of family.[36] In some regions of the United States, especially in the South and in New England, one can still find veritable patriarchal families.

Should it be surprising to learn that these families tend to keep the patrimony within the family, thereby forming true dynasties not unlike the European aristocratic ones? The stability and whatever perdurability exist in American society actually rely on the natural social strati-

---

[34] Alexis de Tocqueville, *Democracy in America* (New York: Penguin, 1956).

[35] "Growing numbers of sociological, historical and psychological studies began to demonstrate not only the existence of defined and cohesive elites in American society, but also that the history of the elites is the principal essence of the history of the country." Plinio Corrêa de Oliveira, *Nobility and the Analogous Traditional Elites* (Hamilton Press, 1993), p. 150.

[36] *Ibid.*," Social Stratification in the United States," pp.145-7.

fication and inequalities that develop organically, as in all sound social orders, the American myth notwithstanding.

The Archbishop of Toledo Poses a Question

In his book on the family,[37] Cardinal Isidro Gomá y Tomás, Archbishop of Toledo, posed a question: What is more in conformance with natural law, the institution of entail and primogeniture or the division of the inheritance of the parents in equal parts to all the children?

His Eminence admitted the difficulty of a categorical response, given the strong reasons both pro and con. Opponents argue that since all children are equal with regard to the love of the parents, the institution of primogeniture is unjust because granting a greater inheritance to one child supposes a greater love. They add that dividing the property makes all the members work more and increases the public wealth. Finally, they argue that these property laws stimulate the class system and the natural development of an aristocracy. Influenced by the egalitarian principles of our age, they see this as an evil.

Taking these arguments into serious consideration, the Archbishop of Toledo nonetheless weighed in on the opposite side:

> "Despite the egalitarian tendency of modern political systems, we believe that, notwithstanding the multiple abuses that take place with the institution of primogeniture, it should prevail over the systematic and equal division of the paternal inheritance." [38]

---

[37] *La família segue el derecho natural y Cristiano* (Barcelona: Casa Editorial, 1952), pp. 292-3.

[38] *Ibid.*, p. 295.

Regardless of the many problems that can arise with family quarrels, the egoism of the first-born, factors jeopardizing the situation of the other children, and so on, Cardinal Gomá y Tomás nonetheless affirmed that the institution of primogeniture, which "perpetuates the customs, traditions, 'air' and spirit of the family, is a great good for the family itself and for society." He continued:

"The family is by nature traditional. It is a society that tends to concentration and durability, because it is a society of love that wants to perpetuate itself. When individuals of a family live together, characteristic ways of acting develop naturally among them, and these are converted into customs peculiar to the household …. When a family lives in *its own* house, with *its own* goods, it will come to form something like a small kingdom, distinct from any other, and will grow, increase and purify itself in the moral order. In time, it will pass this treasure of goods and traditions it has accumulated beyond the boundaries of various generations. We have seen such families in our country [Spain], where the grandfather lives with the grandson, and where the elderly leave behind in the house the memory of a life permeated with the deeds and traditions of those who went before them.

"This is how the spirit of the family is conserved. Some families attach themselves to others, binding themselves by numerous and well-made matrimonies, and by this reach an apex of good customs, faith, patriotism, and an honor without stain. In the good times of these great families, the children who leave the ancestral home can find in it a refuge and support amid the battles of life; if they prosper, they return to it to be rejuvenated on days of feast or sorrow, taking the memories of the life lived in it in order to transplant them into the new branches that have formed and that are becoming, in their turn, other nuclei of traditional life.

"The multiple division of the inheritance brings about the material pulverization of the family. It scatters the treasure of traditions, and suffocates the old spirit of a house, which now sees but one single generation.

"The material ruin is no less in the modern form of wealth. A factory or a business is divided; a more or less forced liquidation can mean economic disaster, and likewise stir up fratricidal quarrels. The land, divided into so many parcels, loses its productive and tax value, with repercussions in the national economy. If the goods are too narrow and the conscience too wide, there can be a fatal drop in the birth rate ...

"Thus, while admitting the essential equality of all the children in the order of their fundamental rights, we judge it more useful for the spirit of the family and the social interest to recognize the rights of first born, who acts as the link in the life and the history of the family, who religiously fulfils the duties toward his brothers that his inheritance imposed on him by the wise provisions of his parents, so that all the family might find in the first-born and in the home place the memory and the action of a paternity that considered the well-being of all in all its provisions." [39]

The notion of preserving and increasing a family home by means of this institution is not so-far-fetched as it may appear at first glance. In many countries, including

---

[39] *Ibid.*, pp. 296-7.

the United States,[40] the father, as head of the family, can reclaim the institution of the right of primogeniture if he judges it better for the prosperity of the family. He can favor the eldest son, which is the most natural, or a younger child who can replace him in his functions of head of the family to assure its stability and well-being. There is a tendency even today to will family businesses to one or more children, and exclude others in order to preserve it.[41]

---

[40] Since the French Revolution, the Inheritance laws of France have applied the liberty, equality, and fraternity policies, providing for the equal division of estates among children, which is difficult to change even through a will. On the contrary, England has had testamentary freedom since the enactment of their Statute of Wills in 1540, and the United States since after the American Revolution. This means that children have no legal rights to any portion of a parent's estate or business if the parent chooses to use a will. A child is only legally entitled to an equal portion of the parent's estate if the parent dies intestate.

[41] Richard and Deborah Stapleton, "Attitudes of Family Business Owners regarding policies for transferring the Wealth of Family Businesses," in Proceedings of the 26th Annual National Entrepreneurship & Small Business Educator's Conference, Patrick H. McCaskey, Ed., Small Business Institute Director's Ass., San Diego, CA., February 2002, pp. 172-7.

It can be surprising to learn that there have always been arguments in favor of variants of the primogeniture and entails system. The re-constitution of such a system can help to restore stability, prosperity, and durability to a traditional family, in the full sense of the word.

*   *   *

Chapter III

PATERNAL AUTHORITY AND MATERNAL GOODNESS
A chapter from the work *L'Esprit familial*
by Msgr. Henri Delassus

If you were to choose the principal characteristic of the father, and also that of the mother, what would they be? What Msgr. Henri Delassus highlighted as essential for a sound family was authority for the father and piety, or goodness, for the mother. In view of the breakdown of paternal authority and the great emphasis placed on careers for mothers in our days, it seems quite timely to reproduce this chapter from Msgr. Delassus' work on the family entitled "The Authority of the Father, the Piety of the Mother, Respect for the Ancestors."

The Authority of the Father, the Piety of the Mother, Respect for the Ancestors

by Msgr. Henri Delassus

The continuity of the family home and the family book are only the material foundation for the existence of a true family. But its vital principle is the authority of father, the piety of the mother, and respect for the ancestors.

The Authority of the Father

In Athens and Rome, the authority of the father was absolute. In his own household, he was a king. He had a truly sovereign dignity and power, and this power extended even to the right of life and death.

In Catholic France, the father never had this right, but he was still the first judge of his children. Up until the 18th century, he conserved the right to deprive an unworthy son of his liberty, even if the latter were of age and married, and the king himself placed his power at the disposition of the father seeking justice. This was what happened when a father asked the sovereign for a *lettre de cachet* (sealed letter),[42] soliciting the assistance of the royal power against a son when the latter was a cause of dishonor to the family. The king could then send him to a State prison. This custom was acknowledged everywhere, even by the receivers of the said *lettres de cachet*.

Paternal authority was considered essentially superior to all others, and, for this reason, profoundly respected. "The prince gives orders to his subjects," says Jean Bodin, "the master to his disciples, the captain to his soldiers ... But to none of these did nature give such authority as to the father, who is the true image of the sovereign God, the universal Father of all things."[43]

---

[42] In French history, the *lettre de cachet* was a letter signed by the King of France and closed with the royal seal, or *cachet*, commanding private actions or judgments. They were often used by the King, at the request of heads of families, as a means of correction to their members, for example, to protect the family honor from the disorderly or criminal conduct of sons. Wives, too, took advantage of them to curb the profligacy of husbands, and *vice versa*.

[43] Jean Bodin, *Les six livres de la République* (Paris: Librairie Générale Française, 1993), book 3, chap. 7.

In fact, children should think of their fathers as images of God upon earth. One frequently finds thoughts like the following, which are those of Stephen Pasquier:

> "We should consider our fathers like gods on earth, who were given to us not only to transmit life to us and conserve it, but also to sanctify us by a wise instruction." [44]

Writing to one of his nieces, St. Francis de Sales affirmed: "Behold how you encounter in your father an image of the Eternal Father. For this reason we should honor and reverence the one through whom it so pleased God to give us life."

An authority with such a religious character should inspire respect and make obedience easy, stimulating devotion to the family and maintaining harmony among the children. Throughout the 18th century, however, paternal authority was deteriorating because of egalitarian new customs, and the National Convention ended by destroying it almost completely.[45]

From the time that men who were imbued with the spirit of Rousseau – that is, men who wanted to see the individual, not the family, as the basic element of society – assumed the legislative power, they strove to enact laws to

---

[44] Étienne Pasquier, *Oeuvres choisies* (Paris: Ed. Firmin-Didot, 1849),

[45] The author is referring here to legislation that robbed the family of its independence by replacing the authority of the father with that of the State. For example, Delassus laments the parent's loss to educate his children: "Today the family depends so much on the State that the father does not even have the liberty to educate his children as his conscience and the traditions of his family indicate to him. The State has taken them from him, with the legally proclaimed objective of transforming these children into men without God, and consequently, men without morals" (chap. 7).

abolish a father's authority over his children older than age 21 and weaken it over those younger. "The imperious voice of reason," proclaimed Cambacérès, a famous revolutionary legislator, "must be heard. Paternal power no longer exists. A man should not have direct power over another, even if it be his own child."[46]

Socialism, in its turn, sought to consecrate these propositions in the law. In his book *Le socialisme intégral*, Benoît Malon said:

> "What must happen is to completely abolish the authority of the father and his almost royal power in the family. In effect, equality only will be perfect if this is achieved. Aren't the children of as great a value as the parents? By what right do the latter command the former? Enough of obedience! Enough of inequality!" [47]

Today, the father finds himself before his children in a situation similar to that of a sovereign deprived of any means to repress the rebellion of subjects. Literature and the media reinforce such laws, working against adults and elders with affirmations that reason belies. Even the schools, through the knowledge transmitted in the order of material facts, persuade the children that they have a true superiority over the parents, who are often ignorant of such learning.

In this way, paternal authority is only a shadow of what it was before the French Revolution. Tocqueville applauded this change:

---

[46] *Moniteur*, August 23, 1793.
[47] Benoît Malon, *Le socialisme integral* (Paris: Ed. Felix Alcan, 1891).

"I think that as the laws and customs become more democratic, the relations of fathers with their sons will become more intimate and affectionate. As law and authority manifest themselves less, confidence and affection will increase. And while it is true that the social bond will weaken, the natural bond will grow stronger." [48]

The facts contradict such predictions, which, moreover, reason cannot admit. Today, everyone deplores the rupture of family bonds and its consequences: the loss of respect and obedience of children toward their parents, the emancipation of the former, the extreme corruption of customs, and finally, the general decadence of the people.[49]

In the upper classes appearances can be better kept,[50] but the reality is no better. Stimulated by the egalitarian doctrine of the age, the youth are revolting frequently against the discipline of the home. More and more their primary concern is to enjoy life in idleness and licentiousness, dissipating the wealth reserved for them by the work of their ancestors.

---

[48] Alexis de Tocqueville, *L'Ancien Régime et la Révolution*, 1866, vol. 2, part 3, chap 8.

[49] In his book *L'Organisation du travail*, Le Play describes this situation and transcribes the pungent testimony left by M. Pénart in a speech given in the tribunal of Douai in 1865, the speech of Gougeau to the Senate on May 23, 1861, and Legouvé's words on the topic in his book *Les péres et les enfants au XIX siècle*.

[50] Henri Delassus was writing these words at the beginning of the 20th century. Today, it can be affirmed without hesitation that a generalized breakdown in the authority of parents is experienced by all classes, not only in France, but in all the countries of Western Civilization, including the United States.

It is, therefore, of pressing urgency to restore paternal authority. No one has a title more legitimate. Nothing is more necessary.

Paternal power is that which, in the natural order, most clearly reveals its divine institution. It is even above the power of the king, which limits itself to directing a society to which one cannot claim rights based in nature. The authority attributed to the father, however, is a legitimate consequence of this natural dignity: that of continuing the work of creation, giving life and new beings gifted with moral consciences and capable of being raised to the knowledge and love of God.

Invested with such high legitimacy, this authority imposes itself by the need to assure the existence of the children, who are powerless to conserve it by themselves. It is imposed by paternal love itself, the most enduring and least egoistic of human affections, because fathers perceive that, without such authority, it would be impossible to educate children who have the stain of original sin. Finally, it is imposed by the service that it renders to society, transmitting through education the treasure of moral truths and experiences accumulated through the centuries. Thus, paternal authority was always and everywhere – except among us at the present hour – considered a foundation stone of the social order, necessary to all peoples and in all times as one of the invariable elements of the social constitution.

Writing about the excellent studies of Le Play on what composes the social body, Charles de Ribbe came to this conclusion demonstrated absolutely by experience: if societies are the image of the families that compose it, families are, in their turn, those in which paternal authority is exercised. He said:

"If we return authority to the father, we will restore the ministry of God in the temporal order .... The more time that passes, the more we become aware that it is necessary to return to the family its autonomy. It is impossible to constitute good governments with men given up to error. In the sad state in which we find ourselves, salvation can only come from that unique authority, which, by virtue of natural law, remains devoted to its subordinates. Only paternal authority can accomplish that which is superior to the force of any public authority." [51]

The Piety of the Mother

The authority of the father should be joined to the piety of the mother.

"Happy the man to whom God gave a holy mother," said Lamartine.[52] He was one who had this happi-

---

[51] Charles de Ribbe, *La société provençale à la fin du Moyen Age* (Paris, 1897).

[52] Alphonse de Lamartine, *Harmonies poétiques*, III, 9, in *Oeuvres de Lamartine* (Paris: Ed. INALF, 1961). Despite his deviations of imagination, Lamartine always treasured the memory of the Christian education his mother gave him. Almost two years before his death, he knelt to receive Holy Communion at the side of his mother at the Easter Mass of the Resurrection. As Joseph de Maistre said: "If it is certain that the mother made it her duty to impress the divine character upon the soul of her son, it is almost certain that the hand of vice will never manage to entirely obliterate that character" (*Considérations sur la France*, Geneva: Ed. Milieu du Monde, 1942).

The memory of a holy mother always accompanies the upright man. Speaking of his mother, Frederick Ozanam, founder of the Conferences of St. Vincent de Paul, said: "When I am good, when I do something for the poor whom she loved so much, when I am in peace with God Whom she served so well, I see that she smiles at me from afar. At times when I pray, it seems to me that I hear her prayer accompanying mine, as it used to do at the end of the day under the Crucifix. Frequently, when I have the happiness to receive Communion,

ness and he never ceased to thank her for "having daily spied out the thoughts of this boy with the end of turning them toward God, just as the source of the running creek is sought, in order to lead it to the fields where it can make the new crop grow." [53]

How many mothers imprint on the souls of their children a respect, worship, and adoration of God, of whom they themselves were, by the purity of their lives, a living image! "My mother," says the poet, "had the piety of an angel. The beauty of her features and sanctity of her thoughts fought together in competition with each other."[54]

The Christian woman, as a mother, sanctifies the child. As a daughter, she edifies the father. As a sister, she helps the brother. As a spouse, she improves the husband.

"I want to make my son a saint," said the mother of St. Athanasius.

"A thousand times thanks, my God, for having given me a holy mother," exclaimed St. Basil the Great, weeping at the death of his mother St. Emilia.

"O my God, I owe everything to my mother," said St. Augustine.

As acknowledgement for having marked him so profoundly with the doctrine of Christ, St. Gregory the Great commanded that his mother Sylvia should be painted at his side. The two fingers of her right hand are extended in a blessing, and her left hand holds the book of the Holy Scriptures.

---

when the Savior comes to visit me, it seems to me that she accompanies Him inside my miserable heart, just as so many times she followed Him when the Viaticum was carried to the houses of an indigent."

[53] A. de Lamartine, *Cours familier de literature. Premier entrétien* (Paris: Ed. Firmin Didot, 1857), p. 9.

[54] *Ibid.*

Who gave us St. Bernard and made him so pure, so strong, so burning with the love of God? His mother, Aleth.

Napoleon himself had to acknowledge, "The future of a child is the work of his mother." And Daniel Lesueur affirmed: "If a person becomes something, it is more often than not due to the mother."

"I owe everything to my father and my mother, who lived so modestly," said Louis Pasteur. "O my valiant mother, you communicated to me your enthusiasm. If I have always associated the grandeur of science with the grandeur of my country, it is because you inspired me with such sentiments."

The saintly Cur of Ars, who loved the life of piety from childhood, accredited his mother for this fact: "After God, I owe this to my mother."

Almost all the saints received the foundation of their sanctity from their mothers.

One can likewise say that great men were formed by mothers.

In a letter directed to Charlemagne, Bishop Cartulfo recalled the Emperor's mother Bertha and said,

"O my King, if God all powerful elevated you in honor and glory above your contemporaries and all your predecessors, you owe this above all to the virtue of your mother!" [55]

---

[55] These mothers saw in their sons that which Lamartine described so well: "*Un serviteur de plus pour servir le Grand-Maître; Un oeil, une raison de plus, pour le connaître; Une langue de plus dans le choeur infini; Par qui, de siècle en siècle, il doit être béni*"

["One servant more to serve the great God, One gaze; one reason more to know Him; One more voice in the infinite choir; By which from age to age He must be praised."]

"It is the bosom of mothers," says Joseph de Maistre, "that forms what is most excellent in the world" [56]

In the home, the mother is that light spoken of in the Gospels that radiates, above all, the light of Faith and the fire of divine charity. It falls to her to nourish in the family the thought of the sovereignty of God, our first principle and our final end, the love and acknowledgment that we should have for His infinite goodness, a fear of His justice, the spirit of religion that unites us to Him, purity of customs, honesty of action, sincerity in speech, devotion, mutual assistance, work, and temperance.

How many families, by means of women, have achieved the highest degree of consideration and prosperity! And how many fallen families were re-instated in respectability through their efforts!

In the 16th century, Louis de Gonzaga was about to enter into bankruptcy. His wife, Henrietta of Cléves, assumed the government of the house and re-established order.... The marriage of St. Jane Frances de Chantal placed her in a disordered household. She began to repair the evil on the very morning following her nuptials. She had the habit of rising very early, and by the time her husband would get up she had already placed order in the house and set the servants to their chores.

In all the social milieus we find similar examples. Augustine Cochin notes:

> "In the families of workers, the dominant figure is that of the wife, that of the mother. Everything depends on her virtue and ends by being modeled by

---

[56] Cartulf, *Instructio epistolaris ad Carolum Regem*, PL, vol. 96, c. 1363.

her. The husband must work and provide for the household. To the wife falls its internal concerns and direction. The husband makes a living; the wife economizes. The husband feeds the children, the mother educates them. The husband is the head of the family; the wife is its link of union. The husband is the honor of the household; the mother, its blessing." [57]

The happy influence of the Christian woman extends beyond the home.

"It was the enthusiasm of mothers and sisters who encouraged husbands and sons to defend the Holy See in Rome. I know of more than one youth who would be enrolled with the Zuaves [the special military body charged with the defense of the Pontifical States] if he had followed the counsels of his mother, but I do not know of one whose mother had impeded him. The father could be weak, but the mother, never: not before, during, or after. A son killed in battle was her pride and when, kneeling before the cadaver of the martyr, God spoke to her in the depths of her heart: "Your son is with Me," gratitude suffocated her sorrow. More than the blood of her son, she loved his glory. [58]

---

[57] Augustin Cochin, *La crise de l'histoire révolutionnaire* (Paris: Ed. Honoré Champion, 1909). See the interesting study by the same author *Les sociétés de pensée et la démocratie* (Paris: Ed. Plon, 1921).

[58] *TN*: This text was written in 1862 about the Zuaves. On September 18, 1860 the main body of the 18,000-man Papal Army was defeated in the battle of Castelfidardo by the revolutionary joint forces that took Rome and the other Pontifical States. The outnumbered Papal defenders put up a spirited and heroic resistance of the papal territories.

"Mary, the model of mothers, had taught these women how one can sacrifice an only son for God and for the Church. Upon hearing the narration of these sublime immolations [of the many French Zuaves defending the Holy See], Pius IX commented, 'No, the France that has produced such saints will not perish!'

"The first time that the heroic widow of the great Zuave Pimodan saw the Pope, she did not say to him, 'Holy Father, return my husband to me.' She said only this, 'Oh! Tell me that he is in Heaven!' When Pius IX responded, 'I no longer pray for him,' she questioned him no more. She understood that she was the widow of a martyr, and this sufficed." [59]

There are few men among us in these last two centuries [18th and 19th] who, even without desiring it, have not made concessions to the Revolution. Women, on the contrary, have the instinct of truth as well as charity. They are inflexible judges before apostasy, betrayal, weakness of spirit. They love the Church and their country, Christ and His Mother. They love them more than themselves, more than wealth, more than their own children. And this love is for them a science. They are the great support of society and the Church. The Revolution knows this also. It knows the number of brothers, sons, and husbands that have been preserved, kept from entering secret societies, by women, even the most simple. The revolutionary is constantly curtailed by this feminine war. Thus their plots to pervert the heart of the woman.[60]

---

[59] Published in *Défense Sociale*, April-August, 1903, under the title "Le progrés,"

[60] *Translator's Note*: The "plots" to gain women that Msgr. Delassus mentions came to fruit with the women's liberation movement that pro-

Respect for Ancestors – The Communion of Saints

The spirit of the family also generates that which was appropriately titled the cult to the ancestors. And it is also nourished by it.

This natural devotion existed in pagan nations, but then degenerated. It still lives in our Christian societies and we see that in China it constitutes a kind of religion.

Among the pagans, this cult to the ancestors began to take shape with the children's natural sentiments of gratitude to the father who gave them life, as well as appreciation for the family whose forebears had given them, not only their material goods, but the lessons and examples of moral virtues that had made the family prosper.

Little by little, to the measure that the years increased that distanced them from the venerated image of the ancestor, this devotion took on a more mysterious aspect and produced in hearts sentiments of a more religious character. This veneration eventually was transformed into a cult properly speaking. The members of a family offered sacrifices to the forebear on his tomb and said to him: "God from the underworld, be propitious to us."

At the same time, an altar was erected on the family hearth. Charcoals burned there night and day, symbolizing the soul of the family, the spirit of the family received from its ancestors and always alive in it. Woe to the house where the hearth fire was extinguished! It could only be put out when the whole family had disappeared.

---

motes the false and ruinous idea that women must be "liberated" from their natural vocation of marriage and maternity. Based on the revolutionary notion of equality, the 20th century introduced innumerable laws that deny the natural hierarchy of the family by establishing equality for men and women in society and marriage.

The extinct fire symbolized the extinct family: they were synonymous expressions.

Christianity destroys nothing that flowers naturally in the human soul, but rather purifies everything. Thus did it also desire that we religiously guard the memory of the authors of our lives, remember and conserve their lessons and examples, and transmit them to future generations.

Even more than this, the Holy Church desires that we remain in communion with our grandparents, with our fathers, mothers, brothers, and sisters who go before us into Paradise. She desires that we pray for them, and that we ask their intercession. She wants us to assist them with prayers and sacrifices, and also that we have confidence in their succor, keeping us on the road upon which they placed us and guiding us by it.

*

Here the admirable chapter of Msgr. Delassus on the authority of the father and the piety of the mother comes to an end.

* * *

Chapter IV

Three Great Social Laws:
Authority, Hierarchy, Union

What would be the greatest enemy of the modern Catholic family? I would say, without hesitation, that it is a profound egalitarianism that is stimulated by progressivist moral principles, supported by revolutionary customs, promoted by civil legislation, and nourished by the educational institutions. It is a profound egalitarianism born from the principles of the French Revolution that wants to make the wife equal to the husband, the children equal to the parents, and the children equal among themselves.

This was not the will of God.

To convince ourselves of the evil of egalitarianism in the family, counsels Msgr. Delassus, it is enough to consider the work of Creation:

"God could have created each man directly as He created Adam, without the help of anyone. He created the Angels in this way. But He did not desire equality among them. He created each angel to constitute an entire distinct species, corresponding to a complete idea. And with them He formed an immense hierarchy, which reflects the richness of divine thinking.

"Since humankind is a single species, equality could have reigned in it .... but God had other plans. He desired that we receive life from other men; thus we are created not in liberty and equality, but in dependence on our parents and in the hierarchy that must arise from this dependence.

"First God created Adam; afterward he gave him as companion a woman, Eve. He then blessed the man and woman and said to them, 'Increase and multiply, and fill the earth and subdue it' (Gen 1:27).

"Thus God created the family. He made it a society, but He followed a plan completely different from that proposed today by social egalitarianism. He desires that the wife *submit* to the husband, and from the children He wants *submission* to the parents.

"We find, then, in the very origin of the human race the three great social laws: authority, hierarchy and union. Authority, which belongs to the authors of life; hierarchy, which confers to man a dominant position in the family and makes the parents superior to the children, and union, which should conserve among them that which is the same life-imparting blood." [61]

What can we deduce from this? *First*, the inequality in the family is rooted profoundly in the designs of Providence. *Second*, this inequality is in itself good and beautiful. It is necessary to be convinced of the essential goodness of the inequality God established in Creation and of the error of the modern egalitarian doctrine that denies this wise order.

Lamentably, strong currents have prevailed in society today that desire complete equality between the sexes. Its partisans proclaim and make laws promoting the supposedly equal duties and rights of the father and mother in

---

[61] H. Delassus, *ibid.*, p.13

the family. With this, the authority in the home is divided. One of the natural consequences of this artificial dual authority in the home is a disharmony that leads to divorce, because if there is no hierarchy, there is no obedience; hence when the two equal parties cannot agree or come to terms, they separate.

I call this situation a natural consequence of egalitarianism because obviously without a head to command, there is division and disorder, and the body, the family, suffers from the resulting confusion.

Already in the 19th century, divorce was supported by revolutionary laws. Paul Bourget, commenting on the French law of 1884 introducing divorce, shows how corrosive it is for the family:

> "The law of divorce was made in the name of the rights of the individual against the bond of the family. It inevitably tends to increasingly corrode those bonds and eventually break them completely. All the motives that were given to authorize divorce will be used to make it more attainable .... I am persuaded that the passage of such laws .... will end in the replacement of the family by the free love union." [62]

A later law made another assault on the husband's authority, lamented Msgr. Delassus:

> "All societies need a head, and the head of the family is the husband. Confirming this truth, the Apostle

---

[62] Paul Bourget, *Essai de psychologie contemporaine,* in H. Delassus, *ibid.*, p. 96. The 1969 Divorce Act enabled no-fault divorce in the United States. The truth of Bourget's prediction on this topic is revealed by today's statistics which show that half of first marriages end in divorce and an ever-increasing number of "partners" living together without marriage.

St. Paul recalled the divine mandate (Eph 5:22-27;
Col 3:18-21). But the new law decided that, regardless of the system adopted by the spouses, the wife
had the power to administer the product of her personal labor and any monies coming from it without
the authorization of her husband." [63]

This judgment against such legislation can sound
harsh to modern ears, accustomed to equal rights jargon
and non-discrimination propaganda. Msgr. Delassus admitted that in cases where women suffered difficult situations, some solution should be found. "But," he added,
"the solution to such private disorders will not be found by
means of violating principles of the social order." [64]

Such violations of the natural law were championed
and introduced in the name of "the higher principle of law,
which is respect for the dignity and independence of the
human person." Based on this principle, progressivist legislation of the last century has continued to corrode the
rights of the family.[65] The stability of the family was destroyed by undermining the authority and hierarchy placed
in it by God

What about the authority of the parents over the
children? Much could be written about the disastrous effects on the children and on society as fathers have gradually lost or surrendered their natural authority. Msgr.
Delassus points to Rousseau, author of the *Social Con-
tract*, as the inspirer for the modern ideas of the "natural
independence" of children:

---

[64] *Ibid.*

[65] Allan C. Carlson describes how the family was gradually stripped of
its economic, educational, and security functions, with the state in most
cases assuming those powers, *From Cottage of Work Station* (San
Francisco: Ignatius Press, 1993), pp. 2-4.,17-24.

"One of the sophisms that Rousseau – mentor of the revolutionary State and evangelist of modern society – derived from the pretended natural goodness of man is this one: 'The children should remain united to the parents only so long as they have need of them to live. As soon as this need ceases, the natural bond is dissolved. The children, released from the obedience they owed to the father, and the father, released from the care he owed his children, return equally to independence. If they remain together, it is not in a natural way, but voluntarily, and the family is then only maintained by convention.'[66]" [67]

This thesis degrades man to the level of animals, exclaimed Msgr. Delassus,[68] indignant over the notion that the bond between a father and child is dissolved as soon as necessity ceases, or that laws can legislate when a child no longer owes his parents obedience.[69]

This sophism that every person should be his own master gave rise to the deleterious spirit of individualism in the family, whereby a child lost not only his sense of

---

[66] Jean-Jacques Rousseau, *Contrat Social ou principes de Droit Politique* (Rouen: Ed. Pierre Dumesnil, 1792) chap. 2, "The First Societies."

[67] Delassus, *ibid.*, p. 95.

[68] *Ibid.*

[69] "In Rousseau there are three themes which have a great relevance to contemporary egalitarianism. The *first* is the virtually nihilistic attitude toward the whole network of social relationships that lies intermediate to the individual and the State .... The *second* theme is the supposed perfectibility of the individual once he has broken loose from the corrupting influences of such social relationships. *Third* is the theme of power, of the necessity of power in the process of extermination of alleged evil traditions and of the moral development of the individual." Robert Nisbet, *The Present Age: Progress and Anarchy in Modern America* (New York: Harper & Row, 1988), p. 116.

duty owed to his parents, but also the responsibility to up-hold their honor and good name.

What the child has lost is much greater than anything gained from this false liberty. He lost the security, seren-ity, and sense of well-being that derived from a well-or-dered and strongly constituted family, the easy capacity to develop his personality and talents in a stable environment of familial community. He became the recipient of the anxieties, unhappiness and instability that result from the family breakdown; he suffered the envy and resentments resulting from the dogma of equality. His moral attitudes became permissive. His supposed emancipation from the "old taboos" of religion and family brought him no peace.

Since the chaos in society flows naturally from the chaos in the family, the solution, by contrast, becomes in-creasingly clear: To restore the family, it must once again be established on the laws of authority, hierarchy and un-ion.

*   *   *

CONCLUSION

This work, the first of a series, is an attempt to facilitate the restoration of the family by showing in Chapter I the very notion of what the family is and how tradition forms its moral soul.

Chapter II pointed to some of the customs and institutions, such as primogeniture and entail, that protected and gave stability to what could be called the body of the family, its house and property that could be passed intact from one generation to another.

Chapter III, which is a literal reproduction of a part of Msgr. Henri Delassus' work, discussed the importance and difference of the roles of father and mother. The parents, in effect, are like a mirror of the Catholic Church for their children. They need to be very pious, serious, kind, patient, and at the same time strong, so that they represent Our Lord Jesus Christ and Our Lady for their offspring. As Msgr. Delassus points out, the father in a particular way must represent authority, and the mother, goodness and sanctity.

Chapter IV dealt briefly with the modern egalitarian conception of family and the need for its restoration on the principles of hierarchy, authority, and union.

At times, seeing the great inroads made by the egalitarian revolution with regard to the family, one might wonder how the destructive process it generated can not only be stopped, but reversed.

Recently a ray of light crossed my path by way of a conversation with an 18-year-old young lady, the eldest daughter of a large family. A short distance away, I could see her parents. Her mother is a housewife who has stayed at home with her children, teaching them, re-assuming the parental right and duty to educate the children. Her father had a confident, calm air, clearly the head of his family.

The daughter, beautiful, composed, with a purity of countenance proper to the feminine ideal, told me she had finished her high school studies.

"What will you do now?" I inquired.

"I'm going to stay home. I can help my mother and set up a little home business with an idea my father and I are working on. I can't imagine going away and living by myself. I love my little brothers and sisters and want to be a part of their lives."

Instead of following the modern fashion to leave home at age 18 to get a job and apartment, or move to a dormitory in a university far from home to assert her "independence," this girl realized the value of being part of a whole, the family, with the protection it afforded to develop her personality.

What this young lady was expressing, without realizing it, was that the life of her family was sufficient for her to fulfill her existence. *First*, she felt that she was fulfilling her filial and fraternal duties. *Second*, she was acquiring the taste for the small pleasures and happiness that a life lived with temperance brings. *Third*, with this unpretentious and joyful way of being, she was preparing herself to be a faithful wife and good mother in the future. *Fourth*, and foremost, she was pleasing Our Lord and Our Lady who had with St. Joseph in Nazareth a simple life like this filled with all the simple and blessed pleasures the family life can bring.

This simple family life, yesterday as today, is born from tradition and founded on the principles of authority, hierarchy, and union. It emerges from a life of sacrifice and courage, lived in a calm and confident environment. That this life is beginning to re-emerge in families offers a hope of a grand regeneration to come.

On this promise of a future regeneration of Christian civilization, Msgr. Delassus has these words:

> "It is true that God at times chastises – and there is a chastisement in the present situation. But it is also true that God does not repent of His gifts. Sooner or later, He will re-place Christendom on the pathways of its youth. And this cannot be too late." [70]

It is my hope that this small book, with the help of Our Lady, will contribute in some way to this restoration.

*   *   *

---

[70] *Ibid.*, p. 165.